Gordon Road Estate
Local and Family History
by
Mary Mason

෨෬

With contributions by
Frances Reed
Lynne Jones
Elise Edwards
David Spreadbury

and

Illustrations by
Teresa Mears

෨෬

Area of interest:
Stanwell Road, London Road,
Gordon Road, Seaton Drive

CONTENTS

Introduction   3

Part One - GORDON ROAD

Early History	4
Census and Valuation Records	7
Directories	9
Parish Registers	10
Gordon Road Residents	11
The Barker Family Tree	13
The Barker Estate	14
Map of the London Road	15
Gloucester Villas - Stanwell Road	16
Previous Ownership of Land	21
Seaton Drive	22

Part Two - "ASHFORD" 1928-58 FRANCES REEDS STORY

The Ashford Home and Bungalow	24
Days in the Garden	25
The Garden Plan	26
The Garden Develops	27
The War Years	28
The Bungalow 1993	29
Conclusions - Moving On	30
Thirty Years On - The Return	32
Gordon Road Today	34
References	35
Name Index	36

ACKNOWLEDGEMENTS

I wish to acknowledge my thanks to the custodians of the public records described in this booklet. They are:-

The Public Record Office, Ruskin Avenue, Kew
The General Register Office of Population Census and Survey
The Greater London Record Office

My thanks also to Marie Newstead for permission to photograph the bungalow in her garden and to David Spreadbury and Elise Edwards for photographs from their family albums.

INTRODUCTION

For a number of years I have been interested in the History of Gordon Road, since we moved here in 1970.

In the main, I have studied the Public Records which are available and added to them details taken from original documents lent to me by other individuals.

My aim has been to record the development of Gordon Road from 1882 until the present day. As often happens with a study of this kind I have found it necessary to extend my original area to include the Stanwell Road and the London Road as my research developed, thus resulting in the title of this book being 'The Gordon Road Estate'.

The Barker family are the main family represented in the book but I have also included details of many other local people as I have come across them.

I am particularly happy to include in part two of the book, "Ashford Story" written by Frances Reed together with reminiscences of Elise Edwards and David Spreadbury, in the first part of the book, which has brought a personal dimension to the book.

My meeting with Frances Reed was quite remarkable, as she now lives in Oban, Scotland but our membership of the West Middlesex Family History Society has united us, together with our interest in local history.

Several people have helped me with their memories of Gordon Road and made useful suggestions, in particular the names I have already mentioned, for which I am very grateful. My thanks also to Reg Sidwell for his "map" of the London Road, to Lynne Jones, Yvonne Woodbridge, Dorothy Copp and John Perkins and special thanks to Teresa Mears for the very fine drawings and Sarah New for her help in design and publishing the book.

Mary Mason
18a Gordon Road
ASHFORD
Middlesex.

August 1993.

EARLY HISTORY

"On or about the 30th January 1882 Arthur Barker was admitted tenant on the parcel of land later to be known as Gordon Road Estates. He constructed a new road and laid out building plots".

This opening paragraph appears on the first page of the Deeds of my house and has prompted me to explore further the history of Gordon Road and trace its development over the years.

A map of 1865 shows Stanwell Road then called Station Road, tree lined with no houses. There are old gravel pits on the Scott Freeman Gardens by the station and the area is very rural.

Continuing from the Deeds the exact location and original size of the plot is described almost poetically. Adjacent land owners and other interested parties make up the picture of this important piece of building land, known locally as 'Parkers Piece'.

> "Situated by Hengrove Pits in Ashford Fields on the North East side of the road leading from Ashford to Stanwell containing by measurement of 8 acres and 26 perches. On the South side by Stanwell Road on the West side by the land formerly of William Sherborn on the North side by a piece of freehold land formerly the property of Elizabeth Lepipre and Peter Lepipre (her son) but later belonging to Anne Graves. And by other enclosures in the Parish of Stanwell and in the East by Glebelands of the Vicar of Echleford otherwise Ashford. And the same piece or parcel of land was finally in the occupation of Thomas Denton or of Henry Ginger and James Ginger"

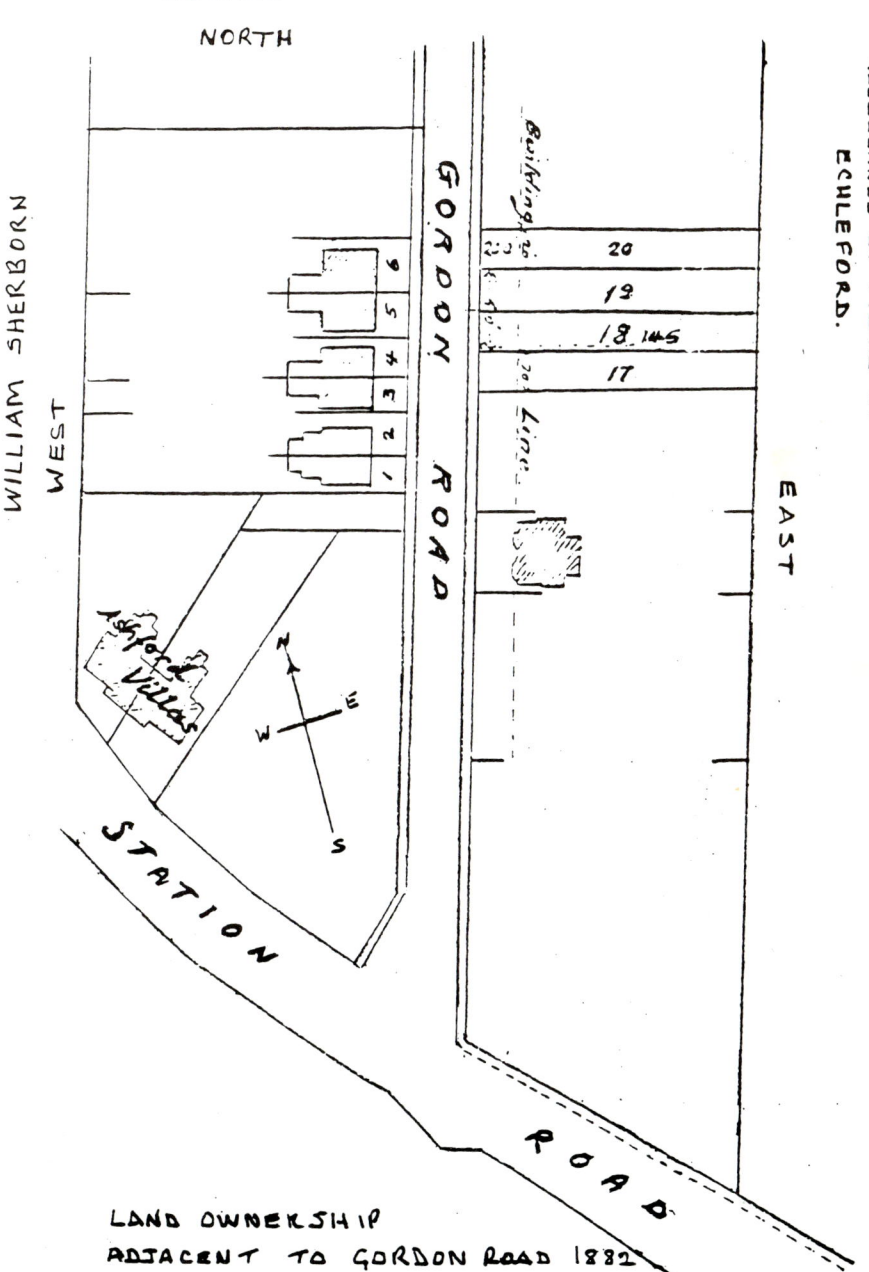

Moving onto 1890/97 much development has taken place, Gordon Road has six cottages on the left hand side and there are eighteen houses on the east side of Station Road (Stanwell Road) known as Gloucester Villas.

This map shows the Stag and Hounds on the London Road with Vine Cottages and a field. The last house in this group is probably Lud Lodge, which shall be described in more detail later. Part of the land by the station is used by the London and South Western Railway, which came to Ashford in 1848. This area is now named after Harry Scott-Freeman, Lord of the Manor of Staines and a prominent solicitor. He left a collection of local history material referring to Staines and Ashford which is now housed in the Greater London Record Office and can be consulted there.

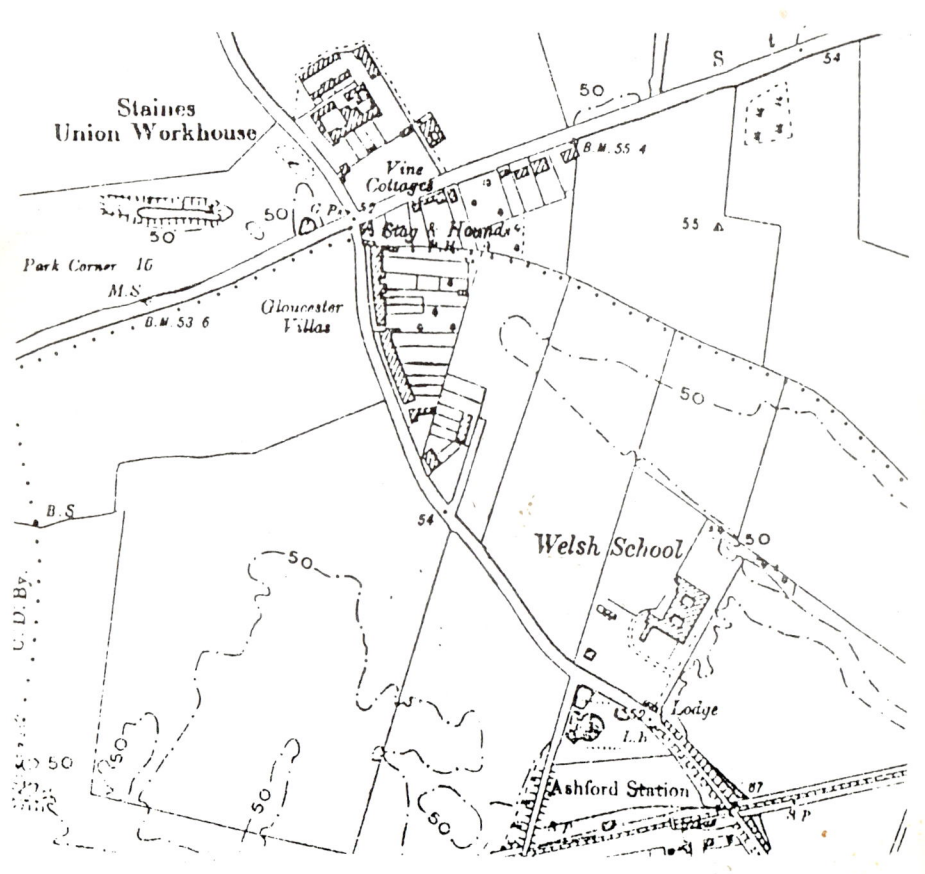

THE CENSUS RETURNS

By looking at the Census Returns taken in April 1881 and 1891, further interesting details may be found. Although Gordon Road does not appear in 1881 census, there are houses on Station Road, namely Gloucester Villas, listing the occupants, giving a guide to when these houses where built. On the 1891 census, Gordon Road has five households but no numbers or house names were shown. These are probably the cottages on the left hand side, now numbered 7 to 17. The residents include a gardener, butcher and a Police Constable

Allan Garrad - Head - 40 - Arthur Garrad - Son - 12
George Lintott - Head - 42 - Butcher and family
Thomas Durham - Head - 28 - Gardener and family
Joseph Spicer - Head - 57 - Surveyor and family
Thomas Bond - Head - 41 - Police Constable

RATE BOOKS

The names and addresses of occupiers and owners of houses in Gordon Road in 1915 and 1921 can be found in the five year samples available. These are divided into six monthly intervals and very little change occurs for the first entries in April and October.

All the house names are given but no map or indication as to the exact location. Unfortunately, the handwriting is very poor and difficult to read. These records can be consulted at the Greater London Record Office.

VALUATION OFFICE RECORDS

Field books 1910 to 1915. For the purpose of making a valuation of all land in the United Kingdom the office was set up under the 1909 Finance Act and valuation began in the whole of England and Wales but was not completed until Autumn 1915. Therefore, some entries are for 1912 and some for 1915.

Houses or parcels of land are listed in a Field book with approximately 100 entries in each book. The information we can find includes the name of the owner of the house and the occupier, which is very important for our purposes, and the type of accommodation which exists e.g. how many bedrooms, sitting rooms, outside toilet and if gas and water is laid on and in particular the actual address of the property which I have not been able to find on the census returns or in the Rate Books. Another useful detail from the field books is a map often found to describe the property and it's relation to other houses in the road.

With the first house in Gordon Road, there is a plan very nicely drawn, showing the cottages on the left, together with eight larger houses and their names. With two exceptions, all the houses are owned by members of the Barker family. The valuation of land indicates various plots owned by residents of Stanwell Road, on the west side the land being used as gardens, orchards or paddock, and 537 foot on the east side owned by A Barker and T G Smith, his son-in-law. See further references to Stanwell Road on Page 16 describing Gloucester Villas.

The valuation of the properties in Gordon Road gives a full description of each house and also notes on the condition of the road. "The road is not yet taken over", presumably by the council "It is not curbed or channelled". I have drawn my own map, linking it with Stanwell Road. The original field books can be seen at the Public Record Office at Kew. Here is an example:-

No.1 Gordon Road dated 13.9.1912
House and Garden
Occupier Mr and Mrs Heskill
Owner Mrs Denton South, 30 Montpelier Road, Brighton
£175 rated value
Three bedrooms (1 small back addition), sitting room, kitchen, washroom, outside toilet, small garden front and rear, water but no gas.
Fair condition.

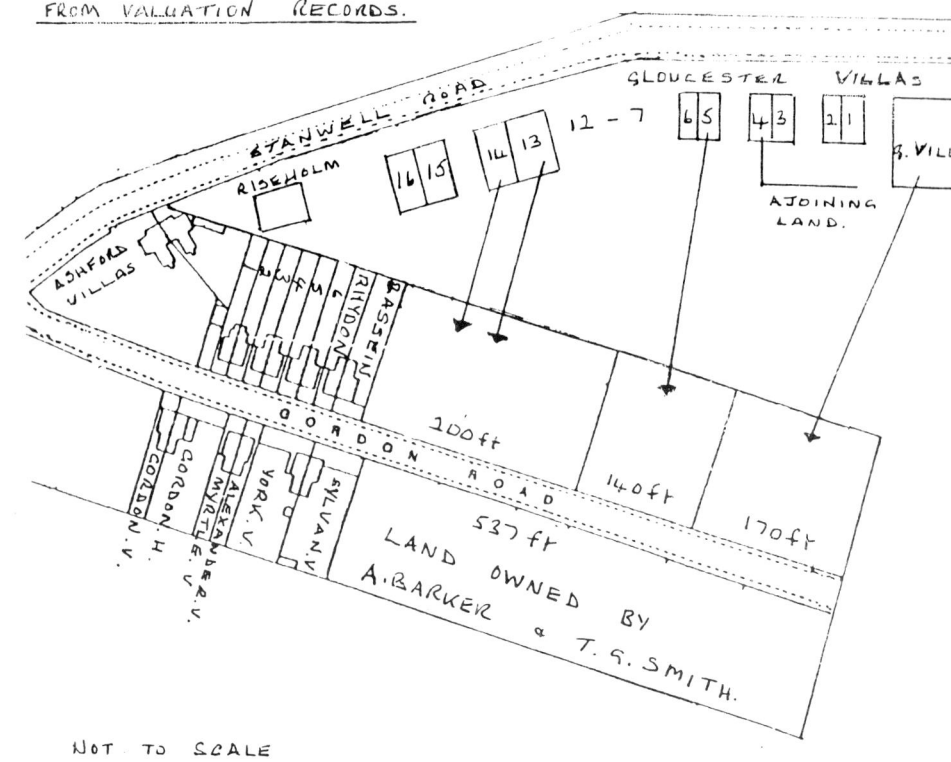

DIRECTORIES

I decided to look in the local Directories for Ashford, Staines and Stanwell and of these Kellys Post Office directories are probably the most well known, published from 1799 to 1939. The early editions list only notable people and tradesmen but later ones have complete roads and names of residents in alphabetical order. A good number of these directories can be viewed at the Guildhall Library and at the Greater London Record Office but nearer to home, Hounslow Library has directories for the years we are interested in - 1874, 1882, 1890 1899 and others from 1903. The 1874 Kellys directory lists all the names of the residents in Gloucester Villas on the Stanwell Road, numbers 1 to 16. Two of these houses will be described in more detail later in the book. The directories also help with estimating when the houses were built. It would seem that Gloucester Villas in 1874 was a very desirable location, because of their position on the main road with open fields at the front and a view almost as far as Staines. Here is a complete list of those living there in 1874:-

GLOUCESTER VILLAS 1874 - *List of names from Kellys Directory.*

1. Charles Hume
2. Jacob Pearce
3. Mrs Collinge
4. Frederick Humphrey
5. John Laidman
6. Mrs Presland
7. Mrs Vincent
8. William Wilbourn
9. Izard Draper
10. Henry Weston
11. James Clements
12. Thomas Young
13. Wyndham Welsh
14. Edward Fenwick
15. Rev Steadman
16. Frederick Woodhouse.

I was able to find Arthur Barker, who developed Gordon Road. He was living at Lud Lodge on the London Road from 1874 to 1891 and his son, Arthur Henry is listed as a builder living in the road from 1908. Gordon Road is mentioned from 1891.

Directories contain notes about the towns' history and origins, such things as posting times for letters and the location of post boxes and details of local schools and churches.

I am grateful to John Perkins at No. 21 Gordon Road who has lent me his copy of Beddows Directory of Staines and District 1947. There are 51 houses in Gordon Road. The old house names no longer survive, only Beaulieu, which is situated at the end of the road.

- 9 -

PARISH REGISTERS

It is surprising what can be found by studying the Parish Registers of Ashford (St Matthews). I was lucky to find a hand written Index of Burials amongst other books in the church, from which I extracted twelve people who had lived in Gordon Road between the years of 1888 and 1917. These include Elizabeth Cannon 1888, Ronald Burt 1895, Charles Fitzpatrick 1896, Elizabeth Maidman 1897, Harold Bennett 1905 from Rhyder Villa and Frances Chapman 1906. Although the actual addresses are not given these could be followed up by looking in the Burial Registers.

Joseph Spicer, a surveyor, lived in Gordon Road and is with his family on the 1891 census. He died in 1909 aged 75 years. Sarah Stokes lived at number 2 in 1903, while Elizabeth Hewitt and her eldest son John are recorded in 1911. There is a memorial to them in St Matthew's Church yard. I am sure more references could be found if time allowed to look through the Baptism and Marriage registers as well. The end of Gordon Road was once in Stanwell Parish so a study of St. Marys Stanwell would also reveal connections with our area.

St. Matthew's Church, Ashford

GORDON ROAD RESIDENTS

The Barker Family

In the opening line of this book I quoted from my house deeds "Arthur Barker Tennant". The Barker family were in fact the most notable family to live in Gordon Road and featured in all the records down the years. Arthur was born in Clapham, London on 20th March 1836 to Henry and Rachel Barker and he married Maria Ann Hills in Cranley, Surrey on the 13th June 1860. She was born in Richmond, Yorkshire and her father was a farmer. I believe they came to Stanwell in 1867 with three young daughters. I found the family on the 1871 census living at Lud Lodge on the London Road.. The house was situated on the south side of the road beyond the cottages and where the new Lud Lodge building now stands and Lodge Way. I do not know exactly when it was demolished but most probably about 1960. I have a description of the house from 1915 Rate Books:-

> "Built of brick and slate, a detached five bedroomed house, 3 sitting rooms, kitchen and scullery, a small conservatory, a bathroom and W.C"

The surrounding land was quite extensive comprising of Orchard, Paddock and gardens. This latter area coming through to form part of Gordon Road and some years later the houses at the end of Gordon Road were built on this spot then in the parish of Stanwell.

The Barkers moved here from Bishop Stortford were Eleanor was born, the two older children where born at Ludgate in the City of London. The census details indicate that Arthur was a prosperous gentleman , the children were educated at home by a governess, he took a liking to the area and decided to buy land.

1871 CENSUS. LONDON ROAD. LUD LODGE

NAME	RELATION	STATE	AGE	OCCUPATION	WHERE BORN
ARTHUR BARKER	HEAD	MAR	35	TOBACCONIST	MIDDX, LONDON
MARIA. A. BARKER	WIFE	MAR	31	—	YORKSHIRE, RICHMOND
ANNE. M. BARKER	DAUR	UNM	9	SCHOLAR AT HOME	MIDDX, LONDON
LILLIE. M. R. BARKER	DAUR	UNM	7	SCHOLAR AT HOME	MIDDX, LONDON
ELEONOR. M. BARKER	DAUR	UNM	5	SCHOLAR AT HOME	MIDDX, LONDON
ARTHUR HENRY BARKER	SON	UNM	3	—	STANWELL
ESTHER BARKER	DAUR	UNM	4 MTHS	—	STANWELL
MARY HILLS	WIFES MOTHER	WIDOW	65	FORMERLY FARMERS WIFE	GUILDFORD, SURREY
EMILY. M. WOODHOUSE	GOVERNESS	UNM	—	—	LONDON

1891 Census

Ten years later the 1881 census for Stanwell records 4 more children in the Barker family 3 sons and 1 daughter. Below is the 1891 census taken on 5th April that year when most of the family were at home. Eleanor had married William Russell, who lived with them. The eldest son, Arthur Henry had joined his father in his business as a Tobacconist and Cigar Merchant.

I would very much like to find a picture of Lud Lodge and to have any information about the house during it's long history.. In 1899, it was used as the Office of Staines Rural District Council, possibly the Engineers and Surveyors department. This continued through to 1915 when the occupier was George W Manning, then during the war it was used as a home for girls.

ಸಿಂಕೆ

1891 CENSUS.		LONDON ROAD.			LUD LODGE	
NAME	RELATION	STATE	AGE	OCCUPATION	WHERE BORN
ARTHUR BARKER	HEAD	MAR	54	TOBACCONIST	CITY OF LONDON
MARIA. A. BARKER	WIFE	MAR	50	—	CITY OF LONDON
LILLI.E M. R. BARKER	DAUR	SINGLE	27	—	CITY OF LONDON
ARTHUR. H. BARKER	SON	UNM	23	TOBACCONIST	STANWELL
ERNEST. A. BARKER	SON	UNM	18	GLOVER	STANWELL
HENRIETTA BARKER	DAUR	UNM	11	—	STANWELL
WILLIAM. R. RUSSELL	SON-IN-LAW	MAR	27	PUBLISHER BOOKS	—
ELEANOR. M. RUSSELL	DAUR	MAR	25	—	CITY OF LONDON

One daughter named Esther, born early in 1871, may have died in infancy. The third son Laurence, born in 1875, only appears on the 1881 census, he may have been away at school in 1891.

BARKER FAMILY TREE

ARTHUR BARKER. = MARIA ANN HILLS. 13.6.1860 CRANLEY SURREY
b 20.3.1836. CLAPHAM LONDON.   b.1841. RICHMOND YORKSHIRE.
d. 4.12.1902. BRIGHTON SUSSEX   d. 31.1.1909 BRIGHTON SUSSEX

ANN. M	LILLIE. M. R.	ELEANOR. M.	ARTHUR HENRY	ESTHER	ERNEST. A.	LAWRENCE. C.	HENRIETTA
27.2.1862	10.4.1864.	b 6.1866	b.1868	b.1871	b.1873	b.1876	b.1880
LONDON	LUDGATE	BISHOP STORTFORD	STANWELL	STANWELL	STANWELL	STANWELL	STANWELL

=

BENTON SOUTH, THOMAS SMITH.   WILLIAM RUSSELL.

THE BARKER FAMILY OF STANWELL LIVED AT
LUD LODGE ON THE LONDON ROAD FROM
1868 to c 1897

THE BARKER ESTATE

Arthur Barker moved to The Causeway, Egham in c1897 to a house called "Belmont" by Avenue Road, which is now demolished since the new Sainsbury's store was built and at present the site is being redeveloped.

He died in 1902 in Brighton and in his will he appointed his son Arthur Henry Barker and his son-in-law, Thomas George Smith to be trustees upon his estate for his wife Maria Ann. His wife out lived him by seven years and in her will, she appointed her eldest daughter Ann Marie South together with Arthur Henry and Thomas Smith to be the executors and trustees.

When reading Arthur Barker's will, it was very interesting to discover just how much property he owned in the area. For this reason I have become interested in a far wider area than the original Gordon Road plot.

It had occurred to me that perhaps each of his children owned one or more houses. This is borne out by the will. To each of his surviving six children he left three houses each in Gordon Road and on the London Road. His two sons also divided the eleven Vine cottages between them. In all Arthur Barker's estate consisted of the following properties:-

On the London Road
Orchard Villas No. 1-6
Apperton Villas No.1-2
Stamford Villa No.1-2
Vine Cottages No.1-11
"Thornleigh" house
Ashford Villas No.1-2 (Stanwell Road)

In Gordon Road
Gordon Road Cottages 1-6
Southleigh Terrace 1-2
Builders Office West Side 20ft x 70ft

The will was drawn up on 17th May 1898. It may be safe to assume that at this date the only buildings in Gordon Road were the six cottages mentioned.

A codicil was added on the 16th September 1901 in which the two houses known as Southleigh Terrace are added and described as "recently erected". The wording continues:-

> "I have recently laid out for building purpose a portion of my land in the Parishes of Ashford and Stanwell and have in part made a new road known as Gordon Road across the said land. And my son the said Arthur Henry Barker has been associated with me in selling, building upon and developing the said land as a building estate. Now I hereby devise to my said son the piece of land upon which he has erected a Builders Office and which is situated on the west side of the said road"

I believe "Southleigh Terrace" could be Numbers 38 and 40 and that the builders office may be behind what is now C.M.A. Polishing which is on the west side of the road just before Number 7. But it has been suggested that this was a coach house belonging to Lud Lodge on the London Road.

Descendants of the Barker family came to live at "Beaulieu" which was built on land across the 'end' of the road about 1913. It was a large bungalow with a considerable amount of land and fine trees. Mr G H Barker lived there with his wife, Lucy Catherine and he died in c1950.

At this time the road did not extend further than the maisonettes at No.60 on the right and the new starter homes on the left. Mrs Barker continued living there until 1964 when the land was sold for development.

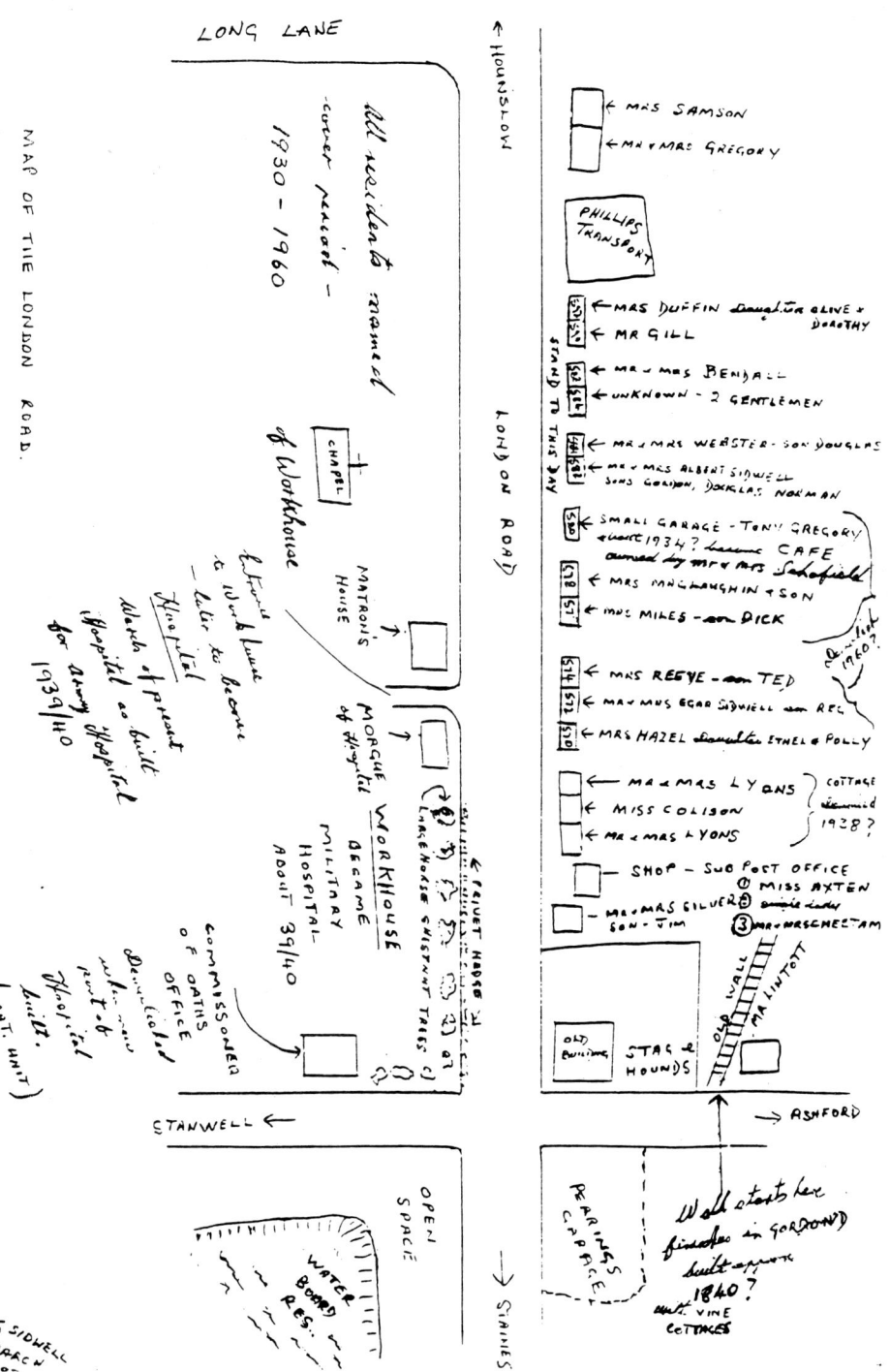

GLOUCESTER VILLAS STANWELL ROAD

In the Valuation Records of 1915, the Gloucester Villas are numbered 1 to 16 and I noticed that land belonging to Numbers 13 and 14 on the Stanwell Road extended through to Gordon Road, a plot measuring 200ft x 165ft (see adjoining map 1934.)

Mr David Spreadbury has told me the history of his house, Number 14 and part of this piece of land. A leasehold document dated 1917 for numbers 3 and 4 Gloucester Villas names the builder as Mr George Cook and the date of construction as 29th September 1866. Each house seems to be slightly different in design. Number 14 which was built in 1863, also by George Cook, had a very fine conservatory at the front and to the right hand side. In the early 1880's, a Mr George Tupman lived there and he built a walled garden which extended right through to Gordon Road. The wall was 6ft high and 10 inches thick and a plaque was erected on each side which read as follows:-

"This wall and 1 foot beyond belongs to Mr George Tupman"

The idea being that nobody would be allowed to place or grow anything up against the wall. There were many fruit trees, a pond and an underground stream. Mr David Spreadbury, has kindly written the following from memory:-

No.14 Gloucester Villas

The house was originally built and the garden laid when all the amenities of today were merely dreams. Water was available only by pumping from the ground, although gas was piped in many years later, at the time, lighting was only possible by oil lamps. Electricity, of course, would have been regarded as science fiction.

An underground stream ran across the bottom of the garden. My sister and I would pump and drink this water. Even during the long hot day of summer it was crystal clear, had a slight earthy taste and was icy cold. It quenched the thirst as no tap water of today could possibly rival.

The bottom part of the garden was sold about 1964. Today there stands a block of maisonettes each with a garage and garden. From memory I think the frontage on the Gordon Road was 60ft and depth about 180ft.

Prior to 1964, this part was mainly the vegetable garden, through the centre portion was a lawn surrounded by trellis, rambling roses, lilac and an arbour of Jasmine screened the lawn from the vegetable garden.

To one side of the lawn was a small building of cement. This had a flight of about ten stairs to a platform about 9ft from the ground, and measured approximately 8ft x 5ft. A door from the lawn led to the garden shed underneath..

On the platform stood a very large water-tank. Its capacity I do not know though the size would be about 5ft long, 4" 6' wide and 4" 6' high. The pump on the lawn was used to fill the tank from the cold stream below the ground.

There the water would slowly warm all the day long until the evening the gravity fed water was used to irrigate the garden. This would be warm, clean and clear water and unsoiled by pollution and chemicals.

At one end of the lawn there was a round pond about 12ft diameter. Around the pond a path and beyond the path again high trellis with Roses and Lilac. In the centre of the pond a mound of bricks and rubble cemented together. From this mound a rotating fountain to fill the pond with clear warm water also from the tank.

As we gradually get older and older, more and more we remember the people and places of our childhood and youth. We can realise how unappreciative we were of our health and happiness and we wish for the impossible. So strange that our memories can hurt us so but without them we would be as nothing.

David Spreadbury
August 1993

As a boy in the 1940's David Spreadbury remembers being sent by his mother to collect goats milk from Mrs Barker at Beaulieu. Instead of walking all the way round he would go through the orchard and climb over the wall dropping into Gordon Road and proceed to the bungalow at the end.

I have examined the wall which now forms the boundary of the gardens and garage area at the rear of the maisonettes in Gordon Road but I have not been able to find the wall plaque. This is because the wall came originally to the pavement and in order to build the maisonettes a section of approximately 30ft was demolished and I am told this section contained the plaque. Clearly visible on the wall are the holes at regular intervals which held metal bars running along at various heights. These were used to support the trees growing against the wall.

The maisonettes were built in 1964 and yet another development built on what must have been a very attractive and interesting piece of land.

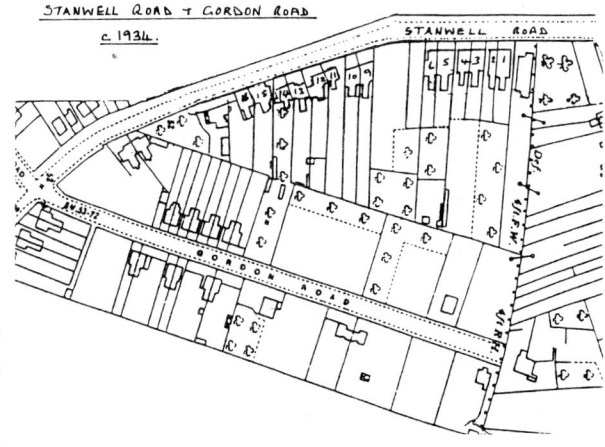

The map c1934 shows Number 14 and the garden extending through and the houses are numbered in their orginal sequence.

This view of the Stanwell Road c1920 is looking towards the London Road and there are very few such views surviving.

Gloucester Villa, the garden and coach house in the 1930's.

The Reed's Bungalow 1934

The children in the garden with Gordon Road houses in the background.

GLOUCESTER VILLA

On the valuation map, land owned by Gloucester Villa is shown which came through into Gordon Road. I am very pleased to include this description by Elise Edwards about the gardens of Gloucester Villa and her recollections of Gordon Road.

My earliest knowledge of Gordon Road was during the war years when my family visited my aunt and uncle, Mr and Mrs Charles Lintott, who lived at Gloucester Villa, 2 Stanwell Road, next to the Stag and Hounds. Their garden reached from Stanwell Road down to Gordon Road and I well remember the happy times spent in this enormous garden as a child.

My family moved from the Berkshire countryside to Ashford just after the war we lived at No.20 Gordon Road, the property of Mrs Barker. At that time No.20 had a large garden at the side of the house as well as extending down to the school boundary. There were two very large horse-chestnut trees in the garden beside the house as well as false acacia's inside the front hedge, and several old fruit trees.

We had access to the Lintott garden through a gate set in the high hawthorn hedge at the end of Gordon Road near the boundary with Mrs Barker's garden. I recall there was also a garden gate between the Lintott and Barker gardens under the cedar tree. My uncle was, I believe, born in Gordon Road before the turn of the century in a house somewhere near No.20 but on the opposite side of the road and the Lintott family would have moved to the house in Stanwell Road very soon after. I remember my uncle telling me that his father bought the extra piece of land on which No.53 and the adjoining properties (No.51 and 55) stand as a playing field for his three sons. According to my deeds this would have been 1899.

The Stanwell Road garden was an absolute delight; we entered from Gordon Road through the garden gate into what was then a grassy area in which my aunt kept geese, then on up the garden path through the vegetable gardens, under an archway in the hedge, past an old brick-built tool shed under the old walnut tree and then onto a beautiful long lawn with fruit trees and herbaceous borders on either side. Then came the fruit garden with a pathway through bordered by flowers on each side, this being where Seaton Drive has now been extended. Then on through another archway with trellis and roses with a rockery the other side onto another lawn with rose trees down each border either side and finally into a rose garden and the terrace and French windows of Gloucester Villa. There was also, to the right of the house and lawn, an old building used for garaging downstairs with workshops above. There was a 6ft high wall down the London Road side of the property which I believe is the Stanwell boundary.

When we came to build the house at No.53 we had to cut through the very old fence and hedge, and I still have pieces of the iron fence which must have been erected in 1899 or thereabouts. "Beaulieu" had already been demolished and Gordon Road extended, with many houses built on the Barker gardens.

Apart from the building of No.53 the rest of the Lintott gardens remained almost as they were first laid out at the beginning of the century and my uncle continued to make his daily pilgrimage the whole length of the garden almost to the day he died at the age of 91.

I sometimes forget the garden is no more. In my memory, it is still there, it is always summer and the roses are in bloom.

Elise Edwards
August 1993

PREVIOUS OWNERSHIP OF LAND KNOWN AS "PARKERS PIECE"

On the first page of this book the piece of land bought by Arthur Barker is described "situated by Hengrove Pits in Ashford fields " etc.

The earliest reference that I have found of this plot is from an Abstract of Title dated 1884. Although difficult to unravel, it has been possible to follow the change of ownership from 1841.

George Frederick Furnival was admitted tennant upon the land at a Special Court in the Manor of Ashford on 28th December 1841. "on the surrender of Casteel Stevens and William Grave together with all buildings", possibly the previous owners.

In his will George left the land to his sons Frederick James and Charles John Furnival and his nephew John Fernival instructing them to sell it by Public Auction of Private Sale.

George died on 7th June 1865 and the land was duly sold on 29th June 1866 to John Thomas Dicks of The Lindens Grove Park Chiswick, a printer and publisher. He paid £1,200 for the said lands and hereditaments therein and was admitted onto the court roll in August of the same year.

In John Dicks' will he left the land to his wife Maria Louisa and sons Henry and John Thomas and James Fenn Beck.

The trustees put the land up for sale by Public Auction as instructed after John Dicks had departed. At the Mart Tokenhouse Yard on 25th October 1881, Arthur Barker was the highest bidder and he paid £1,210 and purchased the land.

On the 30th January 1882, Arthur Barker of 45 Ludgate Hill, City of London, Tobacco Merchant, appeared before Richard Stevens Taylor, Chief Steward at Field Court, Grays Inn (Middlesex) and producing the correct documents "he craved to be admitted tenant on the lands described".

In January 1884, George Tupman of No.14 Stanwell Road bought a piece of land from Arthur Barker to extend his garden into Gordon Road and this is described by David Spreadbury (see page 16).

George Lintott bought land from Arthur Barker on 29th May 1899 which had a frontage on Gordon Road of 170ft as seen in the Valuation Records.

The schedule referred to in the Deed Poll mentions two pieces of land. One in the parish of Ashford, the other in the Parish of Stanwell with the boundary between them measuring 3"6' wide and 312"6' in length. This formed the site of an ancient hedge and ditch and we believe this is the line now taken by the old wall which runs along between Gloucester Villa and the Bulldog.

I am sure there are other conveyances of this sort to be found and I hope some more will be discovered and studied as a result of this book. There are questions left unanswered - why "Parkers Piece" and were there any buildings on the land in 1841?

SEATON DRIVE

Seaton Drive forms a small L-shaped development about two-thirds of the way down Gordon Road. Mr and Mrs Reed gave up their lovely garden in 1958 and this became Seaton Drive and the story is told in part two of this book. Mr Frederick Cast, a builder in Ruislip acquired the land from Mr Reed in 1958, they may have met in Acton as Mr Cast was living there at this time.

He began with the maisonettes No.41 & 43 and continued into Seaton Drive, the bungalows on the left were completed in 1960 with extra land purchased from adjoining gardens and from No.7 Stanwell Road, to make room for back gardens. The Reed's bungalow was preserved and I am sure some of the hedges which divided the plot are still surviving, other walls and buildings which were on the site have been removed. We are still uncertain who owned the next part, on which Mr Cast built the remaining six houses in 1967.

When I moved to Seaton Drive 12 years ago, I was told that our houses were built on gardens from the Stanwell Road and Gordon Road. After pondering over various maps and Mary's search in the District Valuation Books of 1915, the gardens of No.4 Stanwell Road extended behind three adjoining properties (See map page 17). This we feel forms the rectangle in which the six detached houses were built. The house was called FRESNO and was owned by Mr Arthur Moore. It seems likely that the builder bought the land also when it became available but we have no confirmation as yet.

In 1986, after much controversy, 12 starter homes were built. Two blocks of four in Seaton Drive and one block of four in Gordon Road. These were erected on what was originally the end part of the garden of Gloucester Villa and until then grown wild giving shelter to many birds, squirrels, bats and possibly a fox.

It must have been quite strange for Frances Reed pacing out her garden along the paving slabs remembering that here was the pond and there was the rockery and that house was built on the well. She felt her garden seemed bigger than the area she now looked upon. Her one big garden now divided into 18 others.

Lynne Jones
August 1993.

Part Two

Frances Reeds story of her garden in Gordon Road.

ಬಿಂಧ

THE ASHFORD HOME AND BUNGALOW

'Ashford' was bought by my father in 1928. I was very young at the time - but I can remember standing in the empty house which went with the land my father had brought. I believe the house had a name, but to the end of our time there we always spoke of 'going to Ashford' or 'out to Ashford'.

We turned left by the cross roads at Ashford General Hospital and 'The Bulldog' public house, when we first knew it, it used to be called the 'Stag and Hounds' and the hospital was at that time still a workhouse.

The original house still stands on the left of Stanwell Road now No. 12. The previous owner had been a Mr Henry Lock. There was a monkey puzzle tree in the front garden and the land at the rear was a long, comparatively narrow strip opening into a wider part and then into a field through to Gordon Road.

Reminiscing recently, (1988) my mother said that the purchase deal was completed speedily between my father and Mr Lock who already knew each other (probably Smithfield market acquaintances). She said that she was down in their garden having been invited to pick some rhubarb when my father came out and said she could take all she liked as it was now theirs.

After about two years during which we enjoyed numerous days and weekends in the country (yes, it was country then!) the house was sold together with a small area of garden and a 'bungalow' (another misnomer of which more presently) was erected by the new boundary fence. We then entered our property through a gate leading from Gordon Road into the 'bottom' field. In those early days Gordon Road was only a short unmade-up cul-de-sac serving a few cottages and one or two other smallholdings. I think our number was 41 Gordon Road.

The 'bungalow' was simply a one-room wooden building with a sloping corrugated asbestos roof and a balcony from which 4 wooden steps led down to ground level. It was built on 18" high brick pillars to avoid damp. It was painted green with cream window frames and balcony and with flowery chintz curtains hung at the little windows. Through the years it was broken into twice - once by a 'Borstal' boy (the Borstal detention centre was only 2-3 miles away) and once a suspected tramp who took food, a pair of my father's old working trousers and my roller skates - presumbly to sell !

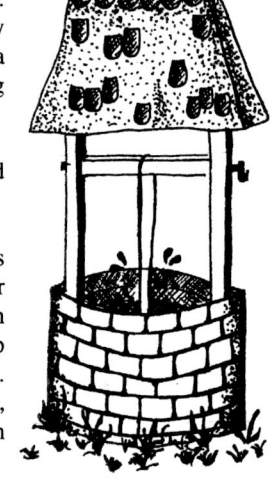

In due course another piece of land was bought and altogether we had about four acres.

My father employed a part-time gardener who worked in the evenings and at weekends. I believe he earned £1 a week in the early days or about 6d per hour for the hours he put in during his spare time. Often Mr Sidwell, our first gardener, brought his young sons with him to help him. He used to cycle round from his house near the 'Stag and Hounds'. The sons, Gordon , Douglas and Norman were older than me - Doug, the younger being about 6 years my senior and to me a big boy . Norman was my own age.

DAYS IN THE GARDEN

In the early years the garden developed to its final form. We had acquired the 'jungle' - about 1/4 acres of land next to the middle part, with numerous old fruit and other trees - Coxes, Pippins, Victoria plum and pear trees. Nothing today compares with that fruit - sun-ripened, picked and eaten straight from the tree, or brought home and stewed or bottled. (There were no household freezers then). Under those trees was long grass which was scythed about twice in a season (I still have one of the scythes!) and in it grew, in due time, bluebells, cow parsley, violets, anemones and other wild flowers. It was a grand place in which to play and hide. It was bounded by an old iron railing but there were 2 or 3 openings and a stile by which the jungle could be entered.

The bottom field also had a number of fruit trees in one half but this grass was kept mown with a motor mower, first a walk behind grass cutter and then a sit on type and latterly by a tractor towing a bigger mower. My father enjoyed tinkering with machinery and on a fine day would be cutting stripes up and down, up and down. I, too, began to drive this before the war as did my mother also. Only once did I 'bark' a tree through inattention. In the square beds under each fruit tree were planted daffodils which gave drifts of gold in springtime. The days spent at Ashford were full of innocent fun and laughter, business and contentment.

Leading from the bungalow was an old parquet flooring type brick path later to be replaced with gravel for easier weeding. (No commercial weed killers were marketed for the public in those days). The path curved and was edged with old red bricks slanted 'dogs-tooth' fashion into the earth.

On each side was a wide herbaceous flower-bed, bordered, in the season with drifts of the old fashioned sweet smelling Mrs Sinkins pinks. There were wall flowers and Sweet Williams, Chrysanths and Russell lupins of all colours, 'Sidwell Daisies' - the gardener introduced them and the name stuck and all sorts of other flowers blooming through the year.

A hazelnut hedge bordered the wide bed on the left, tall and straggly, more a thicket of hazel trees, I suppose, than a hedge. In Spring I loved to find the' lambs tails dangling and especially the less conspicuous little red tufts of the female flowers. I can't remember that we ever had more than a few nuts from them in Autumn.

A white trellis arch led to the middle area where a small round pond was made, with irises and other water plants, including water lillies. Around the rim a narrow bed held spirea plants. A fountain was fixed to play in the middle and goldfish swam in it.

I remember a 'tame' frog which I used to coax into a model rowing boat which I used to sail on the pond. Sometimes he sat there back legs scissored, his front 'fingers' resting on the side of the tiny boat, while I pushed him back and forth across the pond.

The rockery grew from the old rubbish tip - where a previous owner had dumped bricks, old iron and other unwanted articles. The general rubble once the old iron was got rid of, made a good base for the rockery, near which a well was dug from which we could pump ice cold fresh water. There were many gravel pits in the area and there must have been an underground water table.

THE GARDEN PLAN

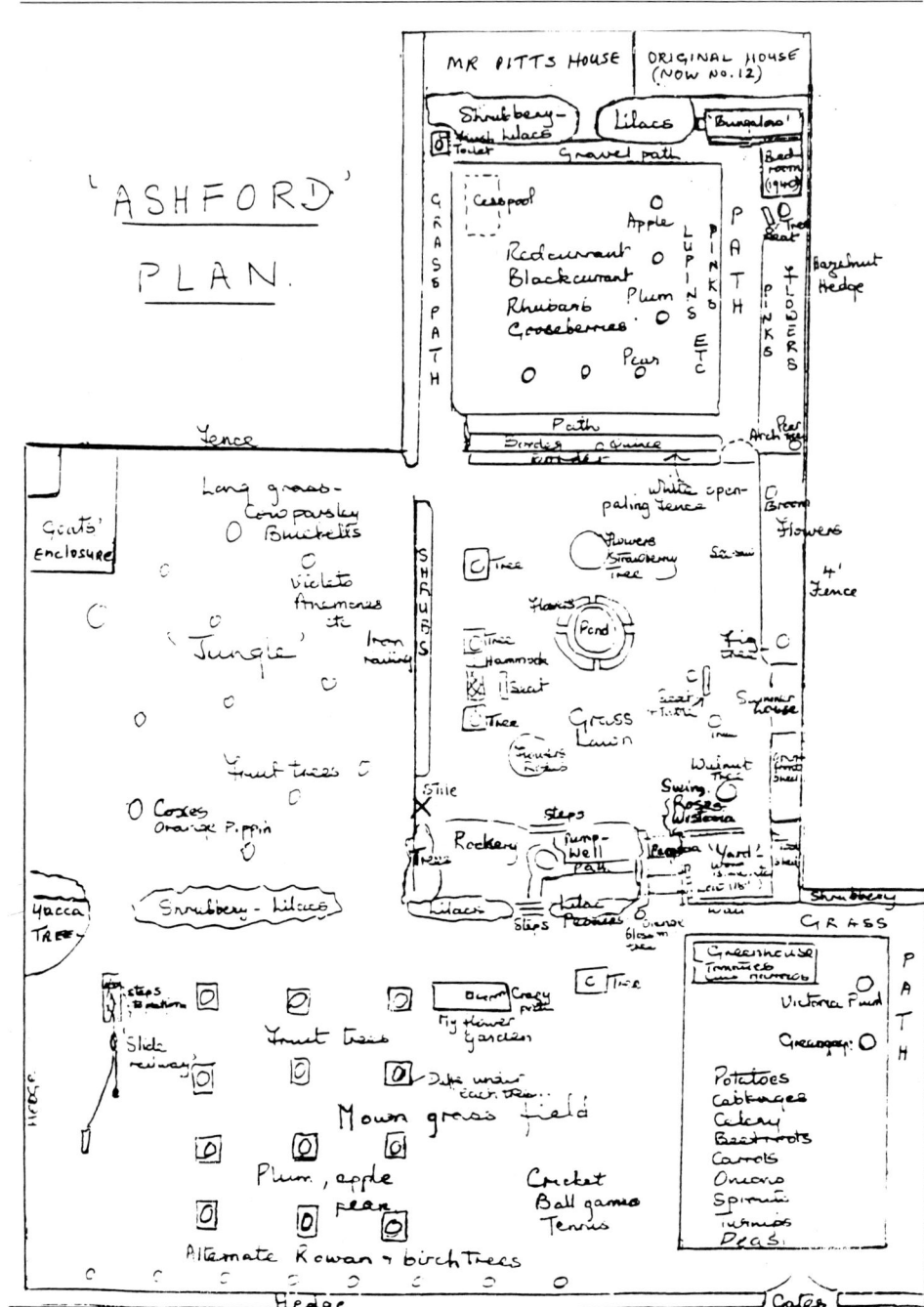

THE GARDEN DEVELOPS

A pergola was built of 4" x 4" timbers leading from the lawn to the bottom field, over which grew a riot of sweet scented rambler roses and I think also a wisteria. Seats were scattered around and we had a hammock between two trees between the pond and the jungle on hot days.

A summerhouse, open fronted sheds and a tool shed completed the side. In the 'yard' - a small square surrounded by a low brick wall planted with aubretia kept all the 'it might come in useful' material, lengths of wood, bricks, pea-sticks and so on. To a child it was guaranteed to provide anything needed for the ploy of the moment. My tricycle, and later a scooter and a bicycle were kept under the open sided sheds, together with the mower, wheelbarrow and a pedal - operated grindstone for sharpening the cycthes and clippers etc. There was also a large grass-roller. There were no vandals, and except for the one incident with the Borstal boy, nothing was ever stolen. The garden tools were kept in the closed shed simply because it was more convenient and there were places for hammer and nails and so on. In the early days nothing was ever locked, not even the bungalow, in pre-war days.

I had a strip of garden in the bottom field to cultivate for myself and had all sorts of things in it, including one year, a giant red poppy with hairy leaves and stems.

After we acquired the 'jungle' a corner was wired off and a small 'house' was erected to shelter two young goats we brought, from a farm on what is now London airport land. They were great fun but when let loose they ate everything, including the daily paper, flowers, clothes off the line - tea towels and so on. Also string, rope, rhurbarb leaves etc. They also 'cornered' people on occasions, and lowered their horned heads and butted!. Agility was needed in order to escape. We tried tethering them but they just chewed through their ropes. Eventually, they were sold to the next door neighbours. Soon, they disappeared from there too.

So the pre-war years passed - all too quickly. Friends came to visit and never went away empty handed - there was always an abundance of flowers, fruit and veges. My own school friends often came with us in two's and three's. There was always a large tea set at the table in the bungalow and we would return home on summer evenings laden with produce, sleepy, happy and full of fresh air.

One day, under a fruit tree near the greenhouse in the bottom field we found 'Little Tortie'. He had wandered and we never found his owner. I already had a 'Big Tortie' - then only about 3" across - so he acquired a companion. During the war I looked after my friends 3 tortoises as well when she was evacuated.

My friends and I played endless games in the jungle and the 'field' among the long grasses. This was, unfortunately, it seems, to be the cause of the distressing hay fever from which I have suffered in varying degrees ever since, every summer.

There was always something to occupy us. At one time, my father rigged up an 'overhead railway' - a kind of wooden tower which was about 12' high and which we climbed by ladder, and from which a cable ran to the ground several yards away. Block and tackle, and, I believe, a rope with which to control the speed, held by an adult, allowed us to hang on and 'cruise' to earth.

THE WAR YEARS

On September 3rd 1939 war was declared. Newly home from Scotland on a blacked-out journey from Aberdeen that had lasted about 18 hours, we snatched a few hours sleep in the early morning before waking to hear Mr Chamberlain(then Prime Minister) make his announcement . Immediately, the sirens wailed (a false alarm as we later discovered) and we packed food, 2 cats (Rusty and Pixie) still mere kittens, Torties and drove straight to Ashford. We deemed it 'safe'. Little did we know.

At first we slept on mattresses on the floor brought from Acton, then we got two double beds into the bungalow room.. My Father and Uncle slept in one, and my Mother and I slept in the other. No finesse - no privacy - and the toilet was along the garden path. After a few nights, Mother and I swopped to sleep head to feet - it gave more room. We bathed in a small galvanised tin bath, boiling up kettles of water on the electric stove - also our only means of heating at first as well as cooking, as Ashford had always been a 'fair weather' place, and we had never slept there after we had given up the original house and I had started primary school.

When somebody took a bath, everyone else went down the garden! I remember one day when my Mother absent-mindedly took the towel with her. Jumping up and down in frustration, as I could hardly run after her, and she was too far away to hear my shout , I dried myself with a yellow duster! For half a term I attended Ashford County School then as the 'phoney' war progressed, we returned to Acton for Christmas.

It must have been at this time that the second room was added, at right, angles to the main room, leading off the balcony. It was here I was to sleep the next time we evacuated from London when the bombing started; and here I had my second attack of measles. When I think of it, I slept in that wooden room for some months, virtually in the middle of a field, as you might say, without even a bolt on the door. No-one dreamed of muggers or rapists then.

When the 'doodlebugs' started to come over, we went to Ashford for a while yet again, often running around the bottom field trying to gauge where the next one might cut its engine and fall and trying to take avoiding action. Luckily (for us) the nearest fell on the hospital , I believe only one person was killed that night. But I am getting ahead of events.

In 1940, came the evacuation of Dunkirk and the news was grim. The weather at that time was as summer ought to be. I seem to remember idyllic days and balmy evenings full of the scent of lilac., and later, orange blossom and pinks and clear turquoise skies shading to lovely sunset colours.

Our meagre petrol ration was eventually Government-augmented, because we had 'dug-for-victory' - a slogan of the time - in the bottom field. Half of it had been dug up and planted with all manner of vegetables. One day, therefore, we were at Ashford. There was a quietness in those days almost unknown today. Until the Battle of Britain Spitfires shattered the skies, and the Wellington bombers started their massive sorties and raids, only the odd single-engine bi-plane or monoplane had sometimes been heard overhead like a distant angry wasp, accentuating the quietness.

The garden at Gloucester Villa and coach house (1958)

The Bungalow as it is today (1993)

CONCLUSIONS

Moving on

On this particular day, however, of sweet summer warmth and stillness, the quietness was undertoned, menacingly. I well remember, though, muted by the distance, the curious sense of reverberation - a ghostly, ghastly rumble, felt - it seemed - as much heard - of the accumulated carcophany of the guns and the fighting from across the channel. The breeze, I suppose, must have been from the East. But nevertheless, that day France and the fighting seemed all too close and real.

Our men, those lucky enough to escape the carnage on the Dunkirk beached, started to come home, and we went to the Willesden railway sidings by an embankment near the 'North Pole' in Kensington, to see them. The troop trains stopped there for a while for some reason, and there was time to exchange greetings with the exhausted, sick-at-heart, and in some cases, injured men. They were grey, drawn, unshaven, stained and battle weary, and many were wearing any clothes they had managed to salvage. I still have a uniform button somewhere that one of the soldiers gave to me, a rather pathetic memento of that time.

I suppose it was a rather morbid curiosity that took people there - us included; but we went too I think with sympathy and support and with a deep gratitude - for the rescue and escape of so many, for their courage and bravery, thought, of course, being British, none of this was expressed in so many words. Only little kindnesses showed peoples' thought, some took drinks - tea, and food for them; cigarettes, beer - their own rations in many cases.

But this story mainly concerns Ashford. The war story is told elsewhere.

After the war, we continued to go to Ashford, though I could go less often because of my spells of duty. However, on days or nights off I was free to go home and we usually fitted in a trip to Ashford.

By this time Gordon Road was 'made up' and one or two more houses and bungalows had been built. There was a pavement and a grass verge with trees along the roadside - red and white hawthorns. But my parents were getting older and even then a 'jobbing' gardener was becoming more difficult to find and keep. An electric hedge-cutter was a great boon as was the tractor towed mower. But time was unfortunately running out for 'Ashford'. The trees - rowans and birches - that we had brought years before from Balmoral and Deeside, and had planted along the inside of the bottom hedge, had grown to be quite large. The garden had a mature air. It was a lovely, familiar place which we had enjoyed for just over a quarter of a century. But there was now a house being built next door to our bottom field and overlooking it. London airport was developing and houses for workers were reputed to be needed. There was talk of compulsory purchase of local land.

I had completed three trainings and was shortly to be off to 'pastures new' in Pendlebury, near Manchester as a Senior Ward Sister and I would be home far less often over the next years. Sadly, it was time to let 'Ashford' go and to sell it privately to a builder was better than having to let it go too cheaply under a compulsory purchase order from the local authority. And so an era came to an end.

Until 1989, I had no idea how the land was 'developed' - what trees were cut down - how many houses were built, or whether any fruit trees were left; the fig tree - the walnut tree - the rowans, the birches? I'd had no wish to go back and find out and I think this may be why my memories are still so clear and untarnished.

Only when I knew that I would be moving away, after my Mother died in August 1989, did I return in order to complete the 'Ashford' story for the family history.

THIRTY YEARS ON

The Return

In the summer of 1989, my mother died just over eighteen months short of her hundredth birthday. I knew that I should eventually be leaving Acton and moving to Scotland. Therefore, on a fine sunny afternoon left over from summer, I made the nostalgic journey - (despite my decision never to return). Turning into Stanwell Road, I couldn't be sure that I had correctly identified the original house, after a lapse of sixty years, as the Monkey Puzzle tree which had stood in its front garden had gone. A number of houses were obviously built more recently than the old row of houses had been, and I could not be sure how near to the corner of Staines Road and 'The Stag and Hounds' it had stood. The Stag and Hounds' I knew had previously been renamed the 'Bulldog' but I saw it was now one of the Harvester chain of restaurants.

Gordon Road was now just another ordinary suburban road, fully made up with houses lining each side. The Hawthorn trees had all gone. Along on the left I found the turning into Seaton Drive in what I thought must have been the approximate position of our entrance gates.

In March 1993, I again revisited Ashford at the invitation of Mary Mason who lives in Gordon Road and at the time of writing was researching the history of the immediate area. I was able to revisit the 'old' bungalow which still stands at the back garden of No.18 Seaton Drive. It appeared dwarfed by the houses now built around it and insignificant in the small garden compared with the old photos and memories of it. On the grass to the left (facing the bungalow) was a rough oblong outline - possibly the site of the old cesspit near to our lavatory. The lilac trees and the old lavatory had long since gone as had the flowers, trees and fruit bushes.

The bungalow (now simply used as a summer house/shed) was in a good state of repair apart from the steps, which had roughly been replaced by cement blocks and paving slabs. The door was all white instead of the cream and green of our day.

It seemed that No.18 had been built on the lower section of the top part of the old garden and the first part of the middle lawn and over the pond area.

The rockery and well are probably now under the concrete of the roadway. The old walnut tree has gone, though I believe a young one is growing now in another garden - possibly a seedling? The old one would have been somewhere under the pavement on the opposite side of the road from No.18

In the front gardens of the houses along our part of Gorden Road, I took a photo looking towards Gordon Road and the houses, showing a section of what must have been our original hedge which ran between the gates leading into the bottom field, and the Lintott bungalow in the next door field. I took another photo from Gordon Road facing the direction of the bungalow which also showed, think, the same section of hedge.

Mary and I walked round to Stanwell Road and saw No.5 (now renumbered No.12) the original house we bought in 1928, next to Mr Pitt (No.6) and I took another photo. We then went on to see the Villas on the London Road, one of which the Sidwells had occupied.

Back in Seaton Drive, we identified in the front garden of the house on the left hand side of the curve in the road, what was most probably one of the original apple trees in the bottom field. There were, possibly, others in back gardens of this and the 'jungle' area.

The surprise of the day was to meet Reg Sidwell, the cousin of Doug and Norman and Gordon, who remembered me and he and his wife live nearby in a street on the far side of Stanwell Road. We had not met or heard of one another for over 50 years! He reminded me of things that I had forgotten among other things of how he too used to come round to the garden with Doug and Norman and their father Bert (Albert) Sidwell, our old gardener. He also said that when we lived in the bungalow when the war came that I used to go round to the Sidwell villa to practise my music on their piano.

Frances Reed
July 1993

London Road cottages

GORDON ROAD TODAY

We have seen that the road comprised of several well laid out gardens and fields, and was once a rural lane turning off Station Road which now seems very hard to believe.

As you come into Gordon Road there are three pairs of semi-detached houses on the right, and one pair on the left passed the original cottages. I think that these were built about 1902 and completed by 1912, probably by Arthur Henry Barker. They are similar in style but when you look closer each pair is slightly different, each having a considerable amount of ground surrounding them and all had names in the 1915 valuation records (see page 8)

As previously mentioned, the pair of large houses opposite the Seaton Drive turning were built about 1900 and called "Southleigh Terrace" in Arthur Barker's will. At least two other houses are shown on the 1934 map. Neighbours have told me of one of these, Mr McCormick's house which was demolished to make way for the maisonettes numbers 54 -60, but unfortunately, I have not been able to find out anything else about these houses.

In 1935, Mr William Wicks built seven bungalows on the land owned by Number 13 Gloucester Villas, part of the plot already mentioned (see map page 8). He was a local builder who started his business in 1931 and became very well known in the area for the bungalows he built, he still lives in Ashford. In 1950 two more bungalows where added on land behind these seven.

Mr Alexander lived at Number 22 and he built a bungalow in his large garden at the side but this was demolished in 1975 to build Wyvern Court and a block of four maisonettes.

Of all the changes and developments that have taken place in Gordon Road the 1960s was a very busy period in the roads history. "Beaulieu" the Barkers bungalow at the north end of the road succumbed to the developers in 1964. Then the road was extended to build the Hewitt & Hillers houses but still fortunately, keeping it as a cul-le-sac. Although I cannot verify this, the cedar tree at Number 65 must have been one of the many trees which surrounded the bungalow. Others have had to be removed. Mr McCormicks house was derelict when the above development took place so in 1965 that was removed to make way for two blocks of maisonettes in 1966.

During the latter half of the 1960's and into the 1970s, houses have been built in between older properties. Number 53 was built on land once owned by the Lintott family on the Stanwell Road, Number 12 was built between Myrtle Villa and Gordon House and 18a and 18b built by Stewart Construction in 1968 in the garden at the side of York Villa.

After a hundred years of growth and development, we have moved from the six cottages on the 1891 census to over one hundred houses in Gordon Road when the 1991 census was taken two years ago, with the addition of Seaton Drive.

As a last historical note, I have found no explanation as to why Arthur Barker called his estate "Gordon Road". The only theory that I have is he named it after General Gordon of Khartoum, who perished in the Sudan on the 26th January 1885. There was a great deal of publicity at the time about General Gordon's plight. Gordon is not a Barker family name so I think there has to be some significant reason why he should choose that name. Has anyone any ideas?.

REFERENCES

Ordnance Survey Maps

Middlesex XIX 6" 2nd Edition 1897 (cover picture)
Middlesex XIX 25" 1864 revised 1934

The Census Returns - for Ashford and Stanwell

1881 Ashford RG11/1325, 1326, 1327
1891 Ashford RG12/1014, Folio 4
1871 Stanwell RG10/1306 Folio 88 Page 17
1891 Stanwell RG12/1017 Folio 96 Page 19

The Public Record Office, Chancery Lane, London WC2A ILR

Rate Books

Ashford   ACC/427/392 dated 26th April 1915
          ACC/427/393 dated 25th October 1915

May also be consulted for 1921 and 1926 making 6 piece numbers in all from 392 to 397.

Parish Registers

St.Matthew's, Ashford and St.Mary's, Stanwell may be consulted at the Greater London Record Office. The above two groups of records are held at:-

The Greater London Record Office
40 Northampton Road
LONDON
ECIR OHB

Monumental Inscriptions for St.Matthew's Church, Ashford can be consulted in Ashford Library, Church Road, Ashford.

District Valuation Records

The Record Class is I.R.58 and the Valuation District is Walton-on-Thames. It is usual to first find the map reference to the area and then consult the Ordnance Survey Map, which for Ashford is XIX 15 and 16 but this valuation map is not available. Therefore I found it necessary to work through the twenty-two books which cover Ashford to find Gordon Road. I have compiled an index of these books that could be of use to anyone using these records. The book numbers for Ashford are 87749 to 87771. Properties in Gordon Road are listed in book 87753 and plots of land 87764 and 87766.

The Valuation Records are held at:-
The Public Record Office
Ruskin Avenue
KEW
Richmond
Surrey
TW9 4DU

NAME INDEX

Alexander 34

Barker 4, 7, 9, 11, 12, 14, 17, 20, 21
Beck 21
Bennett 10
Bond 7
Burt 10

Cannon 10
Cast 22
Chamberlain .. 28
Chapman 10
Clements 9
Collinge 9
Cook 16

Denton 4
Dicks 21
Draper 9
Durham 7

Edwards 20

Fenwick 9
Furnival 21

Garrad 7
Ginger 4
Gordon 34
Grave 21
Graves 4
Heskill 8
Hewitt 10, 34
Hillier 34
Hills 11
Hume 9
Humphrey 9

Laidman 9
Lepipre 4
Lintott 7, 20, 21
Lock 24

Maidman 10
Manning 12
McCormick 34
Moore 22

Parkers 21
Pearce 9
Perkins 9
Presland 9

Reed 22
Russell 12

Scott-Freeman ... 4, 6
Sherborn 4
Sidwell 24, 25, 33
Smith 7, 14
Spicer 7, 10
Spreadbury 16,
South 8
Steadman 9
Stevens 21
Stewart 34
Stokes 10

Taylor 21
Tupman 21

Vincent 9

Welsh 9
Wicks 34
Wilbourn 9
Woodhouse 9

Young 9